AH, LIFE. I
GOT A FEW C.
THIS DOUG.
FEEL FREE TO SHARE!

WITH LOVE

Paul
&
DIANA

A JOLLYTOLOGIST® BOOK

WORKLAUGHS

A JOLLYTOLOGIST® BOOK

WORKLAUGHS

QUIPS, QUOTES, AND ANECDOTES ABOUT MAKING A BUCK

COMPILED BY
ALLEN KLEIN

GRAMERCY BOOKS
NEW YORK

Published by Gramercy Books, an imprint of Random House Value Publishing,
a division of Random House, Inc., New York.

Gramercy is a registered trademark and the colophon is a trademark of Random House, Inc.

Random House
New York • Toronto • London • Sydney • Auckland
www.randomhouse.com

Interior book design by Karen Ocker Design

Printed and bound in Singapore

A catalog record for this title is available from the Library of Congress.

ISBN-13: 978-0-517-22819-7
ISBN-10: 0-517-22819-X

10 9 8 7 6 5 4 3 2 1

CONTENTS

ACKNOWLEDGMENTS

The author wishes to thank the following writers for their contribution to this book:

Laura Stack, author of *Leave the Office Earlier*

Clyde Fahlman, author of *Laughing Nine to Five*

Terry Paulson, author of *They Shoot Managers, Don't They?*

Matt Weinstein, author of *Gently Down the Stream*

Larry Wilde, author of *Larry Wilde's Library of Laughter*

INTRODUCTION

After my daughter, Sarah, graduated from college, she got a job in a well-known stationery store in San Francisco. She liked her job and did extremely well. After about eight months, they made her assistant manager and gave her a raise.

Then one day, shortly after that, she was offered a one-day-a-week job teaching art to children. This was her passion and something she really wanted to do. But the store would not let her take the time off to do it.

Sarah came to me in tears with her dilemma. Should she give up a guaranteed weekly salary in a job which she liked, but had no particular affinity for, or should she quit the job and risk being employed only one day a week?

I told Sarah that I could not make the decision for her because if the outcome was not to her liking, I would be the one to blame. So she would have to make the decision. But I also told her my view of employment—to do what you love to do. It may be hard at first to make ends meet, but if you really love what you do, and work at it, you will become good at it, and people will pay you for your expertise.

Sarah quit the stationery store and took the teaching job. Within several months, she was teaching art classes five days a week at various locations. She has been doing so ever since and is one of the happiest employed people I know.

I hope your work situation makes you happy too. And on those days when it doesn't, I invite you to read some of the material in this book and laugh it off.

ALLEN KLEIN,
SAN FRANCISCO

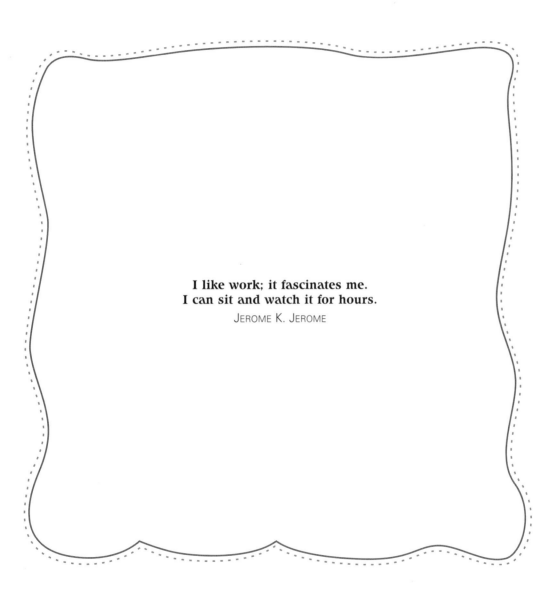

**I like work; it fascinates me.
I can sit and watch it for hours.**

JEROME K. JEROME

NINE TO FIVE

HELP WANTED

GETTING DOWN TO BUSINESS

MINDING YOUR OWN BUSINESS

NINE TO FIVE

Job: a place where you work just hard enough to avoid getting fired while getting paid just enough to avoid quitting.

• • •

Career: a job that has gone on for way too long.

JOE HEUER

If you get to thirty-five and your job still involves wearing a nametag, you've probably made a serious vocational error.

DENNIS MILLER

My father worked for the same firm for twelve years. They replaced him with a tiny gadget this big. It does everything my father does, only much better. The depressing thing is—my mother ran out and bought one.

WOODY ALLEN

I had a boring office job. I cleaned the windows in the envelopes.

RITA RUDNER

Work: The best way to kill time.

EVAN ESAR, *ESAR'S COMIC DICTIONARY*

The world is full of willing people:
some willing to work, the rest willing to let them.

ROBERT FROST

Mankind is divided into two classes, those
who earn their living by the sweat of their brows and those
who sell them handkerchiefs, cold drinks, and air conditioners.

JOEY ADAMS, *THE JOEY ADAMS JOKE DICTIONARY*

Anyone can do any amount of work,
provided it isn't the work he's supposed to be doing.

ROBERT BENCHLEY

When asked how long I've worked here, I replied,
"since the day they threatened to fire me."

ANONYMOUS

There are three kinds of employees: those who make
things happen; those who watch things happen; and those
who have no idea at all what is happening.

ANONYMOUS

It's amazing how long it takes to
complete something you're not working on.

R. D. CLYDE

13

If a thing is worth doing, it's worth doing badly.

G. K. CHESTERTON

**The reason why worry kills more people
than work is that more people worry than work.**

ROBERT FROST

**Millions of people in this country aren't working,
and that is scary. However, the real problem is that
so many of these people are employed.**

RON DENTINGER

HOW TO WASTE YOUR DAY AT WORK

- **Try to phone yourself and hang up fast enough so that it actually rings.**
- **See how long it takes for the electric pencil sharpener to sharpen a brand-new pencil until there's nothing left but the eraser. Repeat until the supply room is out of pencils.**
- **Come in late at night and switch all the nameplates on the doors and cubicles, as that will waste many hours for every one the following morning while people search for the location of their nameplates. Switch yours also and pretend to look with your coworkers.**

BOB SCHWARTZ

All work and no play make Jack a dull boy—
and Jill a wealthy widow.

EVAN ESAR

Every morning I get up and look through the *Forbes* list of the
richest people in America. If I'm not there, I go to work.

ROBERT ORBEN

Conway's Law. In any organization there will always be one
person who knows what is going on. That person must be fired.

PAUL DICKSON, *THE OFFICIAL RULES AT WORK*

The trouble with the rat race is that
even if you win you're still a rat.

LILY TOMLIN

PRISON VS. WORK

- **Prison: Spend most of your time in an eight by ten cell.**
  Work: Spend most of your time in an eight by eight cubicle.
- **Prison: Get time off for good behavior.**
  Work: Get rewarded for good behavior with more work.
- **Prison: Watch TV and play games.**
  Work: Get fired for watching TV and playing games.
- **Prison: Get your own toilet.**
  Work: Share the toilet.
- **Prison: Expenses are paid by the taxpayer with no work required.**
  Work: Pay all expenses to go to work and then taxes are deducted from your salary to pay for prisoners.

ANONYMOUS

Work is the price you pay for money.

ANONYMOUS

**Work is the greatest thing in the world,
so we should always save some of it for tomorrow.**

DON HEROLD

Caught napping at work? Just say:
  "They told me at the blood bank this might happen."
  "Whew! Guess I left the top off the liquid paper."
  "Someone must've put decaf in the wrong pot."
  "Boy, that cold medicine I took last night just won't wear off!"
  "I wasn't sleeping. I was trying to pick up my contact lens without using my hands."

ANONYMOUS

The only thing wrong with getting to work on time
is that it makes for a really long day!

TOM LA FLEUR

When you come in late for work, everybody notices;
when you work late, nobody notices.

RAYMOND F. ELSNER

Take heart! The only person who ever got his
work done by Friday was . . . Robinson Crusoe.

WAYNE B. NORRIS, YOU DON'T HAVE TO BE CRAZY TO WORK HERE . . .

It's true that hard work never killed anybody,
but I figure—why take the chance?

RONALD REAGAN

Tarzan came home from a hard day's work and said:
"Jane, it's a jungle out there."

ANONYMOUS

HELP WANTED

The closest thing to perfection a person ever comes
is when he fills out a job application form.

STANLEY RANDALL

REPLIES TO RESUME QUESTIONS

- **Languages: "Speak English and Spinach."**
- **Reason for Leaving Last Job: "They stopped paying me."**
- **Breaks in Your Employment Career: "15 minute coffee break while working at a home improvement store."**
- **Job Duties: "Planned and held up numerous meetings."**
- **Experience: "I was a CFO for a wholesaler of women's slacks. We also sold men's bottoms."**

RESUMANIA.COM

A businessman of rather shabby reputation was interviewing applicants for the job of chief accountant. He asked each, "How much is two plus two?"

The first two applicants replied, "Four." Neither got the job. The third was hired.

When asked the sum of two plus two, he got up, closed the door, drew the blinds, leaned across the desk and said, "How much would you like it to be?"

RICHARD S. ZERA, *1001 QUIPS & QUOTES FOR BUSINESS SPEECHES*

**You can name your salary here—
I call mine Fred.**

ANONYMOUS

**My consciousness is fine;
it's my pay that needs raising.**

PHYLLIS DILLER

Fresh out of business school, the young man answered a want ad for an accountant. Now he was being interviewed by a very nervous man who ran a small business that he had started himself.

"I need someone with an accounting degree," the man said. "But mainly, I'm looking for someone to do my worrying for me."

"Excuse me?" the accountant said.

"I worry about a lot of things," the man said. "But I don't want to have to worry about money. Your job will be to take all the money worries off my back."

"I see," the accountant said. "And how much does the job pay?"

"I'll start you at eighty thousand."

"Eighty thousand dollars!" the accountant exclaimed. "How can such a small business afford a sum like that?"

"That," the owner said, "is your first worry."

ANONYMOUS

At the end of an interview the Human Resources person asked the young, recent business school graduate, "So what starting salary are you looking for?"

He replied, "I'd settle for around $175,000 a year, provided the benefits package is good."

The interviewer said, "Well, how about 8 weeks vacation, 15 paid holidays, full medical and dental, company matching retirement fund to 60% of salary, and a company car leased every year—say, a Mercedes convertible of your choice?"

The applicant sat up and exclaimed, "Wow! Are you kidding?"

To which the interviewer replied, "Yeah, but you started it."

ANONYMOUS

Interviewer:	"How long did you work at your other job?"
Job seeker:	"Fifty-five years."
Interviewer:	"How old are you?"
Job seeker:	"Forty-five."
Interviewer:	"How could you work 55 years when you are only 45 years old?"
Job seeker:	"Overtime."

ANONYMOUS

Interviewer:	"In this job we need someone who is responsible."
Job seeker:	"I'm the guy you want. On my last job, every time anything went wrong, they said I was responsible."

ANONYMOUS

Quirox was applying for a job. "Now this is the verbal part of your employment test," said the personnel manager. "What does *aurora borealis* mean?"

"It means I don't get this job!"

LARRY WILDE, *LARRY WILDE'S LIBRARY OF LAUGHTER*

3 BIGGEST PROSPECTIVE EMPLOYER LIES

1. This company is very generous with raises.

2. We're all one big happy family.

3. Of course you'll never have to work overtime.

HOWARD SMITH

When applying for a management position, or a job in the corporate sector, you must present yourself as an important business personality, for whom time is money, etc. To accomplish this, have a friend call you in the middle of your interview, and stage a conversation like this:

EMPLOYER: Tell me a bit more about your qualifications.

YOU: Well you see—(ring) excuse me—(answer phone). Talk to me.

YOUR FRIEND: What's up, you wanted me to call you?

YOU: Well tell him he can start looking for a job somewhere else, then.

YOUR FRIEND: What are you talking about?

YOU: 600? No! I need at least 900 and by this afternoon.

YOUR FRIEND: 900 what?

YOU: That's right, and reschedule my appointment with the investor group for Thursday.

YOUR FRIEND: I'm hanging up. (click)

YOU: All right, no more calls for an hour.

ZACK ARNSTEIN AND LARRY ARNSTEIN

How many job applicants does it take to change a light bulb?
Only one, but 200 applied for the job.

ANONYMOUS

WHAT COMPANIES PROMISE AND WHAT IT REALLY MEANS

- *Competitive Salary:* We remain competitive by paying less than our competitors.

- *Join our fast-paced company:* We have no time to train you.

- *Seeking candidates with a wide variety of experiences:* You'll need it to replace the three people who just left.

- *Requires team leadership skills:* You'll have the responsibilities of a manager, without the pay or respect.

- *Problem-solving skills a must:* You're walking into a company in perpetual chaos.

ANONYMOUS

A questionnaire was sent out to vice presidents and personnel directors of the one hundred largest American corporations asking them to describe their most unusual experience interviewing prospective employees. Here are some of the responses:

- A job applicant challenged the interviewer to arm wrestle.

- Candidate said he never finished high school because he was kidnapped and kept in a closet in Mexico.

- Applicant interrupted interview to phone her therapist for advice on how to answer specific interview questions.

LELAND GREGORY

How many people work at this office?
About half of them.

FRED METCALF, *THE PENGUIN DICTIONARY OF JOKES*

24

Lisbeth made an appointment for an interview with a prestigious Colorado corporation. Sitting before the personnel manager, she asked if she could get into the company's well-respected training program.

The pressured exec had been besieged by applications. "Impossible now!" he said. "Come back in about ten years."

"Would morning or afternoon be better?" quipped the ambitious young woman.

LARRY WILDE, *LARRY WILDE'S TREASURY OF LAUGHTER*

MINDING YOUR OWN BUSINESS

The nice part about being in business for yourself is that you can write off so many things—like your free time.

ROBERT ORBEN, *2400 JOKES TO BRIGHTEN YOUR SPEECHES*

Business: Something which, if you don't have any, you go out of.

ANONYMOUS

I love working for myself; it's so empowering. Except when I call in sick. I always know when I'm lying.

RITA RUDNER

The young businessman was just starting his own firm. He rented an expensive office with great views and furnishings. On his first day, he saw a man come into the outer office. Wanting to appear busy, he picked up the phone and pretended he was working on a big deal. He threw around ridiculous figures and made impressive sounding offers. Finally he hung up and asked the visitor, "May I help you?"

The visitor replied, "Yeah. I've come to install the phone!"

ANONYMOUS

"So, what made you decide to go into business for yourself?"
"It was something my last boss said."
"Really, what was that?"
"You're fired."

ANONYMOUS

One particular morning, we were in a rush to get ourselves ready, and the kids up and off to school. John and I were dressed in business attire for a morning meeting with a potential client. We grabbed diapers, blankets, binkies (pacifiers), toys, and headed out the door.

After dropping off the kids, we arrived at the client facility. The receptionist apologetically told us our prospective client was on a call and would be a bit tardy. She ushered us into a conference room to wait, where we sat and read and chatted a bit. John got up to take a look at the view out of the 10th story window, hands in his pockets. At that moment, our client came walking into the room, and loudly said, "Sorry I'm late!" John whirled around, took his hand out of his pocket and out flew a binkie! Somehow the binkie struck the man in the head—creating the ultimate first impression. John stared, horrified, mouth open; I started laughing loudly; the client just looked stunned. We all kind of looked at the binkie, which had safely landed on the conference table, and John said deadpan, "I always carry mine with me."

LAURA STACK

26

Some people who go into business for themselves have more money than brains. But not for long.

ANONYMOUS

Sexual harassment at work,
is it a problem for the self-employed?

VICTORIA WOOD

A father is explaining ethics to his son, who is about to go into business. "Suppose a woman comes in and orders a hundred dollars' worth of material. You wrap it up, and you give it to her. She pays you with a hundred-dollar bill. But as she goes out the door you realize she's given you two hundred-dollar bills. Now, here's where the ethics come in. Should you, or should you not, tell your partner?"

HENNY YOUNGMAN

The owner and proprietor of the crossroads country general store was resisting the enthusiastic sales approach of the aggressive advertising salesman for the county newspaper.

"Young man, this store was started by my grandfather, owned and operated by my father and now by me. Every man, woman and child in the county knows it's here, so why should I advertise?"

"Sir, the church across the street has been there for 75 years," replied the salesman. "But they ring the church bell every Sunday morning."

WILLIAM H. HIGGINBOTHAM

The shopkeeper was amazed when a brand new business much like his own opened up next door and erected a huge sign that read: "BEST DEALS." He was horrified when another competitor opened up on his right, and announced its arrival with an even larger sign, reading, "LOWEST PRICES." The shopkeeper was panicked, until he got an idea. He put the biggest sign of all over his own shop—it read, "MAIN ENTRANCE."

LOWELL D. STREIKER, *NELSON'S BIG BOOK OF LAUGHTER*

OFFICE ROUTINES

MEETINGS & MEMOS

PHONY BUSINESS

LOST IN CYBERSPACE

ON THE JOB

CUSTOMER SERVICE

OFFICE ROUTINES

Office: A business place where you can relax from your strenuous home life.

EVAN ESAR, *ESAR'S COMIC DICTIONARY*

OFFICE RULES

1. The managing director is always right.
2. If the managing director is wrong, Rule One applies.

PETER ELDIN, *JOKES & QUOTES FOR SPEECHES*

RULES OF THE OFFICE

If it rings, put it on hold;
If it clanks, call the repairman;
If it whistles, ignore it;
If it's a friend, take a break;
If it's the boss, look busy;
If it talks, take notes;
If it's handwritten, type it;
If it's typed, copy it;
If it's copied, file it;
If it's Friday, forget it!

DAVID BROOME

We have a rule in our office: The first one to arrive in the morning makes the coffee. Everyone after that complains about it.

GENE PERRET

He and I had an office so tiny that an inch smaller and it would have been adultery.

DOROTHY PARKER

FUN THINGS TO DO AT WORK

- Send e-mail frequently to your supervisor telling him exactly what you're doing. For example: "If you need me, I'll be in the bathroom."
- Whenever the boss asks you to do something, ask her if she wants fries with that.
- Put your trashcan on your desk. Label it "IN."

MATT SILVERMAN, *MY JOB IS A JOKE!*

Do you know what it means to go to an office where you are respected as a human being; where your opinion is appreciated; where your superiors treat you as an equal? It means you've gone into the wrong office.

ANONYMOUS

If it doesn't make any sense, it's company policy!

TOM LAFLEUR

OFFICE LINGO

Cube farm: An office filled with cubicles.

Seagull manager: A manager who flies in, makes a lot of noise, craps on everything, and then leaves.

Ohnosecond: That minuscule fraction of time in which you realize that you've just screwed up BIG time.

ANONYMOUS

Before You Ask for a Day Off, Consider the Following Statistics:
There are 365 days in the year, you sleep eight hours a day making 122 days, which subtracted from 365 days makes 243 days. You also have eight hours recreation every day making another 122 days and leaves a balance of 121 days. There are 52 Sundays that you do not work at all, which leaves 69 days. You get Saturday afternoon off, this gives 52 half days, or 26 more days that you do not work. This leaves a balance of 43 days. You get an hour off for lunch, which when totaled makes 16 days, leaving 27 days of the year. You get at least 21 days leave every year, so that leaves 6 days. You get 5 legal holidays during the year, which leaves only one day, **AND I'LL BE DAMNED IF I'LL GIVE YOU THAT ONE DAY OFF!**

PETE FAGAN AND MARK SCHAFFER, *THE OFFICE HUMOR BOOK*

 Too often I find that the volume of paper expands to fill the available briefcases.

JERRY BROWN

On my first job as a secretary, I made so many typing errors that I spent my whole first paycheck on a briefcase to smuggle out my nine pounds of mistakes at the end of each day.

ESTHER BLUMENFELD AND LYNNE ALPERN

My secretary has a very simple filing system. Everything goes under "L" for "lost." . . . either there or under "S" for "Still Lost."
I said, "If you happen to find something, where do you file it?"
He said, "Under 'W' for 'Will Be Lost Again.'"
I asked, "Don't you have a drawer marked 'F'?"
He said, "Of course. That stands for 'Forget It'."

GENE PERRET

Vicki returned from a coffee break and found her boss gazing dumfounded into the file drawer labeled T – Z.
"Vicky," exclaimed the puzzled man, "where on earth do you keep the Zachary correspondence? This file drawer is completely empty."
"Zachary?" asked the secretary. "Let's see now, is that a company or an individual?"
"What possible difference does that make?" demanded her employer.
"Well, I should say it makes a lot of difference," bristled the girl. "I don't know whether it would be filed under D for Dear Sir or under G for Gentlemen."

LARRY WILDE, *LARRY WILDE'S LIBRARY OF LAUGHTER*

One person's mess is merely another person's filing system.

MARGO KAUFMAN

Looking confused, a new employee with a stack of papers stood before the paper shredder. Walking by, a secretary took pity on him and asked, "Need some help?"

"That would be great," he replied in relief. "How does this thing work?"

"It's simple," she said. Taking a thick report from his hands she fed it into the shredder.

"Thanks," he said gratefully, "but where do the copies come out?"

ANONYMOUS

 Go ahead and destroy those old files, but make copies of them first.

SAMUEL GOLDWYN

Believe me, business should only be as good as office collections. Last week I contributed to five babies, four weddings, three birthdays, and two people leaving. It's ridiculous. I know one woman who hit the jackpot—$8000! She resigned on her birthday when she had a baby while getting married!

ROBERT ORBEN, *2400 JOKES TO BRIGHTEN YOUR SPEECHES*

Did you hear about the company that offered $100 for each money-saving idea submitted by its employees?

The first prize went to the employee who suggested the award be cut to $50.

MATT SILVERMAN, *MY JOB IS A JOKE!*

I was named Employee-of-the-Month for figuring out a tactful way to eliminate the Employee-of-the-Month award.

ESTHER BLUMENFELD AND LYNNE ALPERN

OFFICE ADVICE

- Eat a frog first thing in the morning. Nothing worse can happen to you the rest of the day.
- Never wrestle with a pig. You both get dirty and the pig likes it.
- It is difficult to soar with eagles when you work with turkeys.

ANONYMOUS

One of my co-workers brought his young son to work with him. My friend had warned us that his son was a little shy, so we were all a little surprised to see how eager he was to meet all of us. As the day wore on and it got close to quitting time, I happened to notice how unhappy the youngster appeared to be and I asked him why he was so disappointed. His answer had all of us rolling with laughter. He complained that he never got to see the clowns his dad said he worked with.

CLYDE FAHLMAN

FUN THINGS TO DO
IN THE COMPANY ELEVATOR

- Whistle the first seven notes of "It's a Small World" incessantly.
- Crack open your briefcase or purse, and while peering inside ask: "Got enough air in there?"
- Greet everyone getting on the elevator with a warm handshake and ask them to call you "Admiral."
- Stare, grinning, at another passenger for a while, and then announce, "I've got new socks on!"
- Say "Ding!" at each floor.

ANONYMOUS

A New York City official is in trouble for calling in sick every day for two years. He claims he had a twenty-four-hour bug 730 times in a row.

CONAN O'BRIEN

I finally have a dental plan. I chew on the other side.

JANINE DITULLIO

Doing a good job around here is like wetting your pants in a dark suit. You get a warm feeling but nobody notices.

PETE FAGAN AND MARK SCHAFFER, *THE OFFICE HUMOR BOOK*

PERFORMANCE REVIEWS AND WHAT THEY REALLY MEAN:
- *Approaches difficult problems with logic:* Finds someone else to do the job.
- *Consults with supervisors often:* Pain in the ass.
- *Demonstrates qualities of leadership:* Has a loud voice.
- *Inspires the cooperation of others:* Gets everyone else to do the work.
- *Uses time effectively:* Finds many reasons to do anything except assigned work.

ANONYMOUS

EMPLOYEE EVALUATIONS

- Since my last report, this employee has reached rock bottom and has started to dig.
- This young lady has delusions of adequacy.
- Employee doesn't have ulcers, but he's a carrier.
- Sets low personal standards, then consistently fails to achieve them.
- Employee should go far, and the sooner he starts, the better.
- He's got a full 6-pack, but lacks the plastic thing to hold it all together.
- When her IQ reaches 60, she should sell.
- Donated his brain to science before he was done using it.
- The gates are down, the lights are flashing, but the train isn't coming.
- If you give him a penny for his thoughts, you'd get change.

ANONYMOUS

I have always urged this application of creativity and imagination in our business dealings, especially where people are involved.

A certain greeting card company, however, took this idea rather literally.

An employee whose work had not been satisfactory found a small greeting card in his pay envelope, along with his "Final Check." The card read:

Your work we find, with deep regret,
Is sadly uninspired.
With sorrow tugging at our hearts,
We have to say, "You're Fired."

WILLIAM H. HIGGINBOTHAM

DRAWBACKS TO WORKING IN A CUBICLE

- Being told to "Think outside the box" when you're in a @#$%?*!! box all day long.

- That nagging feeling that if you press the right button, you'll get a piece of cheese!

- You can't slam the door when you quit and walk out.

ANONYMOUS

The brain is a wonderful organ; it starts working
the moment you get up in the morning and
does not stop until you get into the office.

ROBERT FROST

If you don't believe in the resurrection of the dead, look at any office at quitting time.

Robert Townsend

MEETINGS & MEMOS

STANDARD FORMAT
FOR THE BUSINESS MEMO

Always start by saying that you have received something, and are enclosing something. These can be the same thing. For example, you could say: "I have received your memo of the 14th, and am enclosing it." Or they can be different things: "I have received a letter from my mother, and am enclosing a photograph of the largest-known domestically grown sugar beet." As you can see, these things need have nothing to do with each other, or with the point of the memorandum. They are in your memo solely to honor an ancient business tradition, the Tradition of Receiving and Enclosing, which would be a shame to lose.

Dave Barry

Ample locker room space had been provided for several thousand plant employees. But many employees had fallen into the habit of carrying their coats, jackets and sweaters into their work areas so they could go directly to the time clocks at quitting time.

During the summer months this created no problem but when winter set in, the foremen began complaining about the work area being cluttered with coats.

When this problem was presented to me, I asked one of my assistants to write a bulletin board notice, over my signature, requesting that employees use the locker rooms.

Without more than a quick glance, I signed the notice my assistant had written. When it appeared on the plant bulletin boards, my phone never stopped ringing.

"Employees will please leave their clothes in the locker room before going to their work areas."

WILLIAM H. HIGGINBOTHAM

NOTICE:

The coffee machine is out of order today.
Upon request, all employees who will be seriously
affected by this situation will be started with jumper cables.

WAYNE B. NORRIS, *YOU DON'T HAVE TO BE CRAZY TO WORK HERE . . .*

ATTENTION: ALL PERSONNEL
SUBJECT: EXCESSIVE ABSENCES
THE FOLLOWING RULES ARE IN EFFECT:

SICKNESS
Absolutely no excuses. We will no longer accept your doctor's statement as proof, as we believe that if you are able to go to the doctor, you are able to come to work.

LEAVE OF ABSENCE FOR AN OPERATION
We are no longer allowing this practice. We wish to discourage any thoughts that you may need an operation, as we believe that as long as you are an employee here you will need all of whatever you have, and you should not consider having anything removed. We hired you as you are and to have anything removed would certainly make you less than we bargained for.

DEATH (YOUR OWN)
This will be accepted as an excuse, but a two-week notice is required as we feel it is your duty to teach someone else your job.

RESTROOM PRIVILEGES
Entirely too much time is being spent in the restroom. In the future we will practice going in alphabetical order. For instance, those with names beginning with "A" will go from 8:00 to 8:15, "B" will go from 8:15 to 8:30, and so on. If you are unable to go at your appointed time, it will be necessary to wait until the next day when your turn comes again.

PETE FAGAN AND MARK SCHAFFER, *THE OFFICE HUMOR BOOK*

41

NOTICE ABOUT COMPANY EXERCISE PROGRAM

This department requires no physical fitness program:
Everyone gets enough exercise
Jumping to conclusions,
Flying off the handle,
Running down the boss,
Knifing friends in the back,
Dodging responsibility, and
Pushing their luck.

ANONYMOUS

If you had to identify, in one word, the reason why
the human race has not achieved, and never will achieve,
its full potential, that word would be: "meetings."

DAVE BARRY

Meeting: I came, I saw, I concurred.

RICHARD S. ZERA, *1001 QUIPS & QUOTES FOR BUSINESS SPEECHES*

Overheard in a meeting: Please don't think of me as your boss.
Think of me as your friend who is never wrong.

RON DENTINGER

"I'm sorry, he's at a meeting" is the business world's equivalent of
"Not tonight, dear; I have a headache."

GENE PERRET

HOW TO LIVEN UP A MEETING

- Spill coffee on the conference table. Produce a little paper boat and sail it down the table.
- Stay behind as everyone else, including the boss, leaves. Thank them for coming.
- Arrange to have a poorly-dressed young woman with an infant quietly enter the meeting, stare directly at the (male) speaker for a while, burst into tears, then leave the room.

Anonymous

A FUN THING TO DO IF SOMEBODY FALLS ASLEEP IN A MEETING

Have everybody leave the room, then collect a group of total strangers from right off the street, and have them sit around the sleeping person and stare at him until he wakes up. Then have one of them say to him, in a very somber voice, "Bob, your plan is very, very risky, but you've given us no choice but to try it. I only hope, for your sake, that you know what the hell you're getting yourself into." Then they should file quietly from the room.

Dave Barry

Donuts: the only non-negotiable element to a successful meeting.

Joe Heuer

What is a committee? A group of the unwilling, picked from the unfit, to do the unnecessary.

RICHARD HARKNESS

When Charles Kettering, the creative genius of the automobile industry, was told that Lindbergh had flown across the ocean by himself, he said, "It would have been more remarkable if he had done it with the help of a committee."

WILLIAM H. HIGGINBOTHAM

A camel is a horse designed by a committee.

ALEC ISSIGONIS

Having served on various committees, I have drawn up a list of rules:

1. Never arrive on time: this stamps you as a beginner.
2. Don't say anything until the meeting is over: this stamps you as being wise.
3. Be as vague as possible: this avoids irritating others.
4. When in doubt, suggest that a subcommittee be appointed.
5. Be the first to move for adjournment: this will make you popular—it's what everyone is waiting for.

HARRY CHAPMAN

To get something done, a committee should consist of
no more than three men, two of whom are absent.

ROBERT COPELAND

A conference is a gathering of important people who singly can
do nothing, but together can decide that nothing can be done.

FRED ALLEN

We just bought a new conference table. It's eight
feet wide, thirty feet long, and sleeps twenty!

ROBERT ORBEN, *2500 JOKES TO START 'EM LAUGHING*

Business conventions are important because they demonstrate
how many people a company can operate without.

J. K. GALBRAITH

A young buyer from Des Moines, in Chicago for a convention,
filled out her first hotel registration card this way:

Name: Selma Hansley
Address: 806 Oak St., Des Moines, Iowa
Firm: Not very.

LEO ROSTEN, *LEO ROSTEN'S GIANT BOOK OF LAUGHTER*

PHONY BUSINESS

We don't care. We don't have to. We're the phone company.

LILY TOMLIN AS ERNESTINE THE OPERATOR, "LAUGH-IN"

I don't understand. I went on a two-week vacation. When I got back to the office there were four weeks of phone calls waiting for me.

GENE PERRET

BUSINESS CALL
**When you make a business call
And the secretary says,
"Will he know what this is regarding?"
Just tell her, "Not unless he's clairvoyant."**

CARMEN RICHARDSON RUTLEN

"Information. Can I help you?"
"I'd like the telephone number of the Theater Guild, please."
"One moment, please." Pause. "I'm sorry, sir. I have no listing for Theodore Guild."
"No, no. It isn't a person. It's an organization. It's the *Theater Guild.*"
"I told you, sir, I have no listing for a Theodore Guild."
"Not Theodore! *Theater*! The word is theater! T-H-E-A-T-E-R!"
"That, sir, is not the way Theodore is spelled."

JOE CLARO, *THE RANDOM HOUSE BOOK OF JOKES & ANECDOTES*

"Who's calling?" was the answer to the telephone.

"Watt."

"What is your name, please?"

"Watt's my name."

"That's what I asked you. What's your name?"

"That's what I told you. Watt's my name."

A long pause, and then, from Watt, "Is this James Brown?"

"No, this is Knott."

"Please tell me your name."

"Will Knott."

Whereupon they both hung up.

LEWIS AND FAYE COPELAND, *10,000 JOKES, TOASTS & STORIES*

**That's an amazing invention,
but who would ever want to use one of them?**

RUTHERFORD B. HAYES (IN 1876, AFTER WITNESSING
A DEMONSTRATION OF THE TELEPHONE)

I wrote a letter to one company complaining about their voice-mail system. I said, "Please, can't I talk to a rational, logical, thinking, feeling human being?" They wrote back and said, "We don't have any people like that working here."

GENE PERRET

THE NEW CELL PHONE LINGO

Buzzerk: The panic people experience when they can't get their cell phones out of their pocket in time.

Celbotomy: Not having any common sense when you use your cell phone.

Cell envy: The constant need to upgrade your cell phone.

Cellfoolery: Pretending to speak on a cell phone in order to appear important to others.

Cellsymphony: The sound of musical ring tones going off during a public performance.

ANONYMOUS

"If you'd like to press 1, press 3. If you'd like to press 3, press 8. If you'd like to press 8, press 5 . . . "

• • •

" . . . If you'd like to pass the time by speaking to someone else who's on hold, press 4."

RANDY GLASBERGEN (CARTOON CAPTIONS)

For a list of all the ways technology has failed to improve the quality of life, please press three.

ALICE KAHN

LOST IN CYBERSPACE

I believe there will be a world market for approximately five computers.

THOMAS WATSON (PRESIDENT, IBM, 1943)

The great Technion Institute in Israel perfected an electronic translator, a machine that could with blinding speed render the text of any one of twenty-two languages into any one of the others.

The marvelous machine was returned to the laboratory for improvement when this sentence from the New Testament was fed into it:

The spirit is willing, but the flesh is weak.

—and this answer, in Russian, popped up:

The vodka agrees, but the meat smells bad.

LEO ROSTEN, *LEO ROSTEN'S GIANT BOOK OF LAUGHTER*

Guthery's Observation: In an evolving man-machine system, the man will get dumber faster than the machine will get smarter.

SCOTT B. GUTHERY

My computer is so fast. Before yours can boot up, mine has already crashed three times.

BILL JONES

If Bill Gates had a penny for every time I've had to reboot my computer . . . Oh my God, he does!

FRED METCALF, *THE PENGUIN DICTIONARY OF JOKES*

YESTERDAY

Yesterday,
All those backups seemed a waste of pay.
Now my source files have all gone away.
Oh I believe in yesterday.

Suddenly,
There's not half the files there used to be,
And there's a milestone hanging over me.
The system crashed so suddenly.

I pushed something wrong
What it was I could not say.
Now all my data's gone
and I long for yesterday-ay-ay-ay.

Yesterday,
The need for backups seemed so far away.
I knew my data was all here to stay,
Now I believe in yesterday.

ABCSMALLBIZ.COM

I work in a busy office, and when a computer goes down it causes quite an inconvenience. Recently one of our computers not only crashed, it made a noise that sounded like a heart monitor. "This computer has flat-lined," a co-worker called out with mock horror. "Does anyone here know how to do mouse-to-mouse?"

ANONYMOUS

Our company has a giant abacus.
It's for emergencies in case the computer breaks.

MILTON BERLE, *MILTON BERLE'S PRIVATE JOKE FILE*

I don't know anything about computers.
I don't even know how often to change the oil.

BUZZ NUTLEY

A large insurance company had installed a powerful new computer to do most of the office work. Of course nobody could fix it when it crashed, so they called in a consultant. He took only a few minutes to examine the machine. He then took out a hammer, tapped the side of the computer and it immediately started again.

Then the consultant handed the office manager a bill for $1,050.

"This is outrageous," the manager said. "All you did was tap on the damn machine with your hammer!"

"Read the bill more carefully," the consultant replied, handing it back to the manager. He took the bill and read, "Tapping the computer carefully with the hammer $50. Knowing where to tap—$1,000!"

ANONYMOUS

A woman called [a] help desk about a problem with her printer. The tech, wanting to know what operation system she was using, asked the simple question, "Are you running it under Windows?" The woman paused and then said, "No, my desk is next to the door, but that's a good point. The man sitting in the cubicle next to me is under a window, and his is working fine."

LELAND GREGORY

Click *here* for the fun of clicking.
Click *here* to see an image of a hand with its index finger pointing.
Click *here* 100 times for carpal tunnel syndrome.
Click *here* 1,000 times really fast to sound like a cricket.
Click *here* if you want to donate a cup of rice to a poor child.
Click *here* for the poor child's address and a map so you can find your way to the poor child's house and give him/her their cup of rice.
Click *here* if you'll be bringing a salad or side dish.

MARC JAFFE

Computerize: What you get when you stare at a video display terminal for more than twenty minutes.

DIANE LOOMANS AND KAREN KOLBERG

YOU SPEND TOO MUCH TIME ON THE COMPUTER IF
- You know more E-Mail addresses than you know telephone numbers.
- Your Internet Provider is Down or Busy and you can't think of anything to do.
- You send yourself E-Mail instead of writing yourself a note.

ANONYMOUS

ERROR MESSAGES
- "The world will end in 5 minutes. Please log out..."
- "Bad Command or File Name. Good try, though."
- "Press any key... no, no, no, NOT THAT ONE!"
- "Hit any user to continue."
- "Smash forehead on keyboard to continue."

ANONYMOUS

COMPUTER BLUES
(or Gone with the Wind)

My document is near perfect,
Concise and well-paced,
Then one wrong command,
And oops—it's erased.

ALLEN KLEIN

To err is human. But in order to really foul
things up, you need a computer.

ANONYMOUS

In a few minutes a computer can make a mistake so great
that it would take many men many months to equal it.

MERLE L. MEACHAM

COUNTRY-WESTERN COMPUTER LINGO

- *Log-on*—Make the wood-stove hotter.
- *Log-off*—Don't add any more wood.
- *Monitor*—Keeping an eye on the wood-stove.
- *Download*—Getting the firewood off the pickup.
- *Megahertz*—Happens when you're not careful downloading.

ANONYMOUS

Computers are definitely smarter than people. When have you ever
heard of six computers getting together to form a committee?

• • •

Computers will never replace man
entirely until they learn to laugh at the boss's jokes.

JOE GRIFFITH, *SPEAKER'S LIBRARY OF
BUSINESS STORIES, ANECDOTES AND HUMOR*

MAKOWER'S IMMUTABLE LAWS OF COMPUTING

- You will never run out of disks or printer ribbons during business hours.
- No matter how long you delay your purchase of a computer product, a faster, cheaper, and more powerful version will be introduced within forty-eight hours.
- If you back up a disk, the original is guaranteed not to fail.
- Printers are not intended to work the first time you set them up. If they do, it is because you didn't follow instructions.
- You never lose data you don't need.

JOEL MAKOWER

HARDWARE: Where the people in your company's software section will tell you the problem is.
SOFTWARE: Where the people in your company's hardware section will tell you the problem is.

DAVE BARRY

Data Processing Law: On a clear disk you can see forever.

PAUL DICKSON, *THE NEW OFFICIAL RULES*

HIGH TECH COMPUTER SALES JARGON

New: Different color from previous design
Designed simplicity: Manufacturer's cost cut to the bone
Field-tested: Manufacturer lacks test equipment
Direct sales only: Factory had big argument with distributor
Maintenance-free: Impossible to fix
All solid-state: Heavy as Hell!
High reliability: We made it work long enough to ship it

ANONYMOUS

How many computer engineers does it take to change a light bulb?
Why bother? The socket will be obsolete in six months anyway.

MATT SILVERMAN, *MY JOB IS A JOKE*

The real danger is not that computers will begin to think like
men, but that men will begin to think like computers.

SIDNEY HARRIS

The only reason that computers can do more work than
people is they don't have to stop to answer the phone.

PAUL HARLAN COLLINS, *2500 GREAT ONE-LINERS*

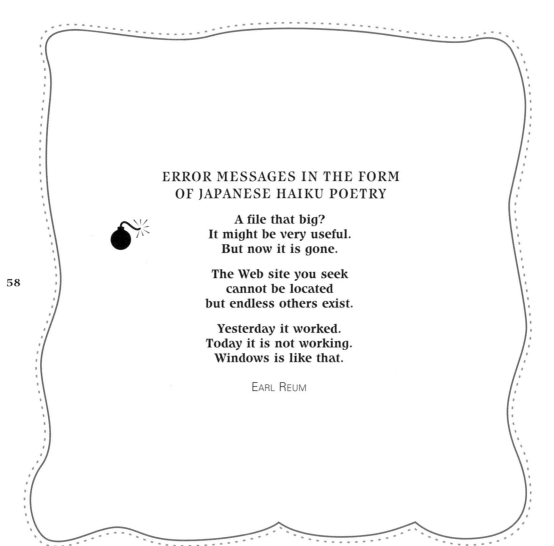

ERROR MESSAGES IN THE FORM
OF JAPANESE HAIKU POETRY

A file that big?
It might be very useful.
But now it is gone.

The Web site you seek
cannot be located
but endless others exist.

Yesterday it worked.
Today it is not working.
Windows is like that.

EARL REUM

Attention spam: the time it takes to decide
whether an e-mail is worth reading.

JOE HEUER

CUSTOMER SERVICE

Complaint department: whine merchant.

PAUL HARLAN COLLINS, *2500 GREAT ONE-LINERS*

The Harmon and Hutson Store, in business for ten years, decided to celebrate the appearance of its one-millionth customer. As a Mrs. Celia Matsill entered the store, cameras flashed, the officers applauded, the publicity department released balloons, and Messrs. Harmon and Hutson piled gift packages, chits for merchandise, and a complimentary order for a year's supply of household goods into the ample arms of the startled Mrs. Matsill. And as the camera of the local television station rolled, a reporter asked the lucky lady, "And what did you come into Harmon and Hutson's for today?"

Said Mrs. Matsill, "The complaint department."

LEO ROSTEN, *LEO ROSTEN'S GIANT BOOK OF LAUGHTER*

An employee at a retail store saw a customer struggling with an armful of items. Trying to be helpful, he asked if the patron wanted a shopping basket. Her reply was, "Don't you think I've got enough to carry already?"

LELAND GREGORY

QUESTIONS TO THE AT&T CUSTOMER SERVICE OPERATOR

Customer: Can you tell me if my calling card is in my wallet?

• • •

Operator: To place a call, you just dial 1-800-OPERATOR.

Customer: How do you spell "operator?" I'm not a math wizard, you know.

• • •

Operator: Is this an average size bill for you?

Customer: I think so...it's usually around 3" by 5".

ANONYMOUS

Phone call from an elderly woman to a pharmacy:

"Can you call my doctor and see if there is another medication he can prescribe for me? The metal foil on those suppositories really hurts!"

• • •

Wal-Mart Employee (on phone): Thank you for calling your Wal-Mart Supercenter. How can I help you today?

Customer: How late are you open?

Wal-Mart Employee: We're open twenty-four hours, ma'am.

Customer: Okay, so what time do you close?

LELAND GREGORY

Sometimes I envy undertakers.
They only have to deal with the customer once.

GENE PERRET

ODD JOBS

THE WORK FORCE

DOLLARS AND SENSE

ODD JOBS

Accountants:

Accountants work their assets off.

Bumper sticker

**I was an accountant. I wasn't a very good accountant.
I always felt that if you got within two or three
bucks of it that was close enough.**

Bob Newhart

**Our Accounting Department is the office that has the little red
box on the wall with the sign saying: IN CASE OF EMERGENCY,
BREAK GLASS. And inside are two tickets to Brazil.**

Robert Orben, *2500 Jokes to Start 'Em Laughing*

Athletes:

**It's just a job. Grass grows, birds fly, waves
pound the sand. I beat people up.**

Muhammad Ali

When Joe Louis was asked who had hit him the hardest during his boxing career, he replied, "That's easy—Uncle Sam!"

ANONYMOUS

BANKERS:

A banker is a person who is willing to make a loan if you present sufficient evidence to show you don't need it.

HERBERT V. PROCHNOW

The drive-in bank was established so the real owner of the car could get to see it once in a while.

ANONYMOUS

A bank teller didn't recognize me. He said, "I need to see two pieces of ID, Mr. Sledge." So I tore my driver's license in half.

TOMMY SLEDGE

A lot of people will urge you to put some money in a bank, and in fact—within reason—this is very good advice. But don't go overboard. Remember, what you are doing is giving your money to someone else to hold on to, and I think that it is worth keeping in mind that the businessmen who run banks are so worried about holding on to things that they put little chains on all their pens.

MISS PIGGY

**No matter how much the boss likes you,
if you work in a bank you can't take home samples.**

EDDIE CANTOR

**Banker, to an assistant, during a robbery: A robbery—
oh thank heavens! I thought it was an unfriendly takeover.**

JOE GRIFFITH, *SPEAKER'S LIBRARY OF
BUSINESS STORIES, ANECDOTES AND HUMOR*

BUREAUCRATS:

Bureaucrat: A red tape worm.

EVAN ESAR, *ESAR'S COMIC DICTIONARY*

Dealing with bureaucracy is like trying to nail jelly to the wall.

JOHN F. KENNEDY

**Bureaucrats are the only people in the world who
can say absolutely nothing and mean it.**

JAMES H. BOREN

Q: How many bureaucrats does it take to change a light bulb?

A: One to spot the burned-out bulb, his supervisor to authorize a requisition, a requisition typist, twelve clerks to file requisition copies, a mail clerk to deliver the requisition to the purchasing department, a purchasing agent to order the bulb, a clerk to forward the purchasing order, a clerk to mail-order, a receiving clerk to receive the bulb . . . .

PAUL DICKSON, *JOKES*

Trying to get some information about her Social Security account, Shephard talked on the phone first with a clerk, then a claims representative, then a supervisor, and finally a district manager. After all those phone calls, she still knew no more than when she had begun.

In desperation, she e-mailed her congressman to see if he could get something done. The reply was a form letter that said "Thank you for your letter of support. I encourage you to visit our nation's Capitol to see your government in action."

Furious, she replied, "In action? In action! First, someone's going to have to tell me if that's two words or one."

JOE CLARO, *GET A LAUGH!*

CAB DRIVERS:

I don't know what it's like to drive a cab. It must be very difficult, because they're very upset, these people. And sometimes you just want to lean over the seat and go, "What is happening in your life and your mind that is making you drive like this? Take it easy."

JERRY SEINFELD

Too bad that all the people who know how to run the country are busy driving taxicabs and cutting hair.

GEORGE BURNS

CLEANERS:

Window sign: We do not tear your clothing with machinery. We do it carefully by hand.

ANONYMOUS

CONSULTANTS:

After the ship has sunk, a consultant knows how it might have been saved.

NEWT HIELSCHER

A consultant is someone you pay a hundred
dollars an hour to give you the same advice
you ignore from your assistant.

ROBERT ORBEN, *2400 JOKES TO BRIGHTEN YOUR SPEECHES*

Construction Workers:

A young man at a construction site always bragged that he was
stronger than everyone else there. He would especially make fun
of one of the older workmen. After a while, the older man had
had enough. "Why don't you put your money where your mouth
is?" he said. "I'll bet a week's pay that I can haul something in
a wheelbarrow over to that building that you won't be able to
wheel back."

"You're on," the braggart replied. "Let's see what you got."

The old man reached out and grabbed the wheelbarrow by the
handles. Then, nodding to the young man, he said with a smile,
"All right. Get in."

ILANA WEITZMAN, EVA BLANK, AND ROSEANNE GREEN, *JOKELOPEDIA*

Three crews were competing for a contract with the telephone company. In order to select the most qualified, the phone company instructed each crew to go out and see how many telephone poles they could erect in one day. At the end of the day the first crew reported thirty-five poles to the phone company official, who was obviously impressed. "Good, but not good enough," he told the second crew, who had installed thirty-two. "Well?" he asked, turning to the third crew. "Two," said the foreman proudly. "So why are you so proud of yourself? Those guys did thirty-five and those did thirty-two," he said, pointing to the other crews. "Yeah," said the foreman, "but look how much they left sticking out of the ground."

LOWELL D. STREIKER, *NELSON'S BIG BOOK OF LAUGHTER*

How many carpenters does it take to screw in a light bulb? Hey! That's the electrician's job!

ANONYMOUS

DENTISTS:

I think I've got to find a new dentist. The only diploma mine has on the wall is from his high school drill team.

ROBERT G. LEE

A dentist at work in his vocation
always looks down in the mouth.

GEORGE PRENTICE

If God meant us to eat sugar
he wouldn't have invented dentists.

RALPH NADER

Doctors:

Q: How many doctors does it take to change a light bulb?

A: That depends on whether or not it has health insurance.

PAUL DICKSON, *JOKES*

It is a good idea to "shop around" before you settle on a doctor.
Ask about the condition of his Mercedes. Ask about the competence
of his mechanic. Don't be shy! After all, you're paying for it.

DAVE BARRY

There was a time when an apple a day kept the doctor away,
but now it's malpractice insurance.

ANONYMOUS

A young doctor was complaining to an older colleague, "Every time I attend the weekly meeting of my service club somebody gets me in a corner and starts pumping me for free medical advice. It's embarrassing, but I don't know how to prevent it."

"No problem," the old timer said. "I figured that one out years ago. When anyone does that to me, I stop him with one word—'undress.'"

WINSTON K. PENDLETON, COMPLETE SPEAKER'S GALAXY OF FUNNY STORIES, JOKES AND ANECDOTES

Sign in doctor's office:
Doctor is real busy. Please have your symptoms ready.

ANONYMOUS

My father is a doctor, with the worst handwriting.
He wrote me a note once excusing me from gym class.
I gave it to my teacher, and she gave me all of her money.

RITA RUDNER

ECONOMISTS:

**A study of economics usually reveals that the
best time to buy anything is last year.**

MARTY ALLEN

ENTERTAINERS:

**I should have been a country and western singer.
After all, I'm older than most western countries.**

GEORGE BURNS

Sherry, one of thousands of unemployed actors in New York City,
sat in the anteroom of a photographer's studio, waiting for her pic-
tures. A young man came in, sat opposite her, and struck up a conversation.

"What kind of work do you do?" he asked.

"I'm an actor," she said.

"No kidding?" he beamed. "Which restaurant?"

JOE CLARO, *THE RANDOM HOUSE BOOK OF JOKES & ANECDOTES*

Help Wanted Ad:
Girl wanted to assist magician in cutting-off-head illusion.
Salary plus medical coverage.

ANONYMOUS

FACTORY WORKERS:

I used to work in a fire hydrant factory.
You couldn't park anywhere near the place.

STEVEN WRIGHT

Help Wanted Ad:
Man wanted to work in dynamite factory.
Must be willing to travel.

ANONYMOUS

FARMERS:

If a parsley farmer goes bankrupt, can they garnish his wages?

BRUCE BAUM

Help Wanted Ad: Man to take care of cow
that does not smoke or drink.

ANONYMOUS

Gas Station Attendants:

I love the way everybody is getting fancy job titles. Gas station attendants are now called "petroleum consultants." They saunter over. "I'd recommend the 89 octane unleaded. It's an unpretentious little fuel with a surprising kick. Would you care to sniff the nozzle?

ROBERT G. LEE

I saw a sign at a gas station. It said "help wanted."
There was another sign below it that said "self-service."
So I hired myself. Then I made myself the boss. I gave
myself a raise. I paid myself. Then I quit.

STEVEN WRIGHT

Auto Repair Sign:
"Free pick-up and delivery. Try us once,
you'll never go anywhere again."

• • •

Sign outside a muffler shop:
"No appointment necessary. We hear you coming."

• • •

Tire shop sign:
Invite us to your next blowout.

ANONYMOUS

Grocery Clerks:

Q: How many grocery store cashiers does it take to change a light bulb?

A: Are you kidding? They won't even change a five-dollar bill.

PAUL DICKSON, *JOKES*

There's a smart young man working in the produce section of a large supermarket when a big, mean-looking customer interrupts him and says, "I'd like half a head of lettuce."

And the young clerk looks at the guy and says, "Sir, we can't sell half a head of lettuce."

But the customer, who's a big burly guy, insists, so the clerk tells him he'll check with the store's manager.

He finds the store manager and says, "Mr. Abernathy, there's some blithering idiot in the produce department who wants to buy half a head of lettuce." Just as he finishes his statement, he turns and sees that the customer has followed him and is standing right in back of him. So the young clerk turns back to the store manager and says, "And this gentleman wants to buy the other half."

SOUPY SALES, *STOP ME IF YOU'VE HEARD IT!*

Why is it that in 7-Eleven stores they've got $10,000 worth of cameras watching twenty cents' worth of Twinkies?

JAY LENO

LANDLORDS:

THREE BIGGEST LANDLORD LIES

1. Just tell us what you don't like about the apartment, and we'll have it all fixed up before you move in.

2. Don't worry about what it says in the lease; we'll always let you sublet.

3. This is definitely a very secure building; there's no way a robber can get in.

HOWARD SMITH

LAWYERS:

A lawyer is a person who writes a 10,000-word document and calls it a brief.

FRANZ KAFKA

How many lawyers does it take to change a light bulb? Three: Two to argue the question of whether the bulb is permanently burned-out or is only temporarily disabled by being turned off, and the third to judge the issue, based on whether the public currently favors darkness or light.

PAUL DICKSON, *DICKSON'S JOKE TREASURY*

"Are you a lawyer?"
"Yes, I am."
"How much do you charge?"
"A thousand dollars for four questions."
"Isn't that pretty steep?"
"Yes, it is. What's your fourth question?"

JOE CLARO, *GET A LAUGH!*

Whoever said talk is cheap never hired a lawyer.

WAYNE MACKEY

A corporate executive received a monthly bill from the law firm that was handling a big case for his company. It included hourly billings for conferences, research, phone calls, and everything but lunch hours. Unhappy as he was, the executive knew that the company would have to pay for each of these services. Then he noticed one item buried in the middle of the list: FOR CROSSING THE STREET TO TALK TO YOU, THEN DISCOVERING IT WASN'T YOU AT ALL—$125.

JOE CLARO, *THE RANDOM HOUSE BOOK OF JOKES & ANECDOTES*

THREE BIGGEST LAWYER LIES

1. I won't charge you for this meeting.
2. Don't worry, I have the judge in my pocket.
3. If we have to go to trial, we'll win hands down in front of a jury.

HOWARD SMITH

If law school is so tough, how come there are so many lawyers?

CALVIN TRILLIN

MAIL CARRIERS:

If you're tired of life in the fast lane,
get a job at the post office.

PAUL HARLAN COLLINS, *2500 GREAT ONE-LINERS*

Did you know that bills travel through the
post at five times the speed of cheques?

CHARLES DOLLEN

THE POSTMAN

Not gloom of night nor sodden ground
Stays him from his appointed round.
He slogs through rain and sleet and hail
To bring me someone else's mail.

JOYCE LA MERS

MEDICAL SPECIALISTS:

We're living in an age of medical specialists. Nowadays what
four out of five doctors recommend is another doctor.

ROBERT ORBEN, *2400 JOKES TO BRIGHTEN YOUR SPEECHES*

Dermatologists make rash judgments.

PATRICIA MAJEWSKI

Sign in a gynecologist's office: "Dr. Jones, at your cervix."

• • •

Sign on a maternity room door: "Push. Push. Push."

ANONYMOUS

A male gynecologist is like an auto
mechanic who has never owned a car.

CARRIE SNOW

An optometrist was instructing a new employee on how to charge
a customer. "As you are fitting his glasses and he asks how much
they will cost, you say, 'Twenty-two dollars.' Then, you hesitate
for a few seconds and watch his eyes carefully. If his eyes don't
flutter, you then say, 'For the frames. The lenses will be fifteen
dollars.' Again, you pause and look into his eyes. If they still don't
flutter, you say, 'Each.'"

WINSTON K. PENDLETON, *COMPLETE SPEAKER'S
GALAXY OF FUNNY STORIES, JOKES AND ANECDOTES*

Sign in an optometrist's office: "If you don't see what
you're looking for, you've come to the right place."

ANONYMOUS

You can't fully comprehend the phrase "million-dollar
smile" until you've had a child in orthodontic braces.

JEAN WALTER

Pediatricians are men of little patients.

SHELBY FRIEDMAN

I had a guy tell me he was a plastic surgeon, and he has two kids. That must make the "daddy's got your nose" game a little scarier.

Paula Poundstone

Sign in a plastic surgeon's office: "We help you pick your nose."

Anonymous

Painters:

John got a job painting the strips down the center of the highway. His first day he dipped his brush into the bucket and was able to paint a whole mile of lines. The second day he painted half a mile. The third day, he painted a quarter of a mile. On the fourth day John's boss showed up and asked, "How come each day you seem to paint less and less?"

   "Well, sir," John replied, "each day I get farther and farther from the can of paint."

Anonymous

PLUMBERS:

A lawyer called a plumber to fix a leaky faucet. The plumber eventually arrived, and after about ten minutes of work the faucet had stopped dripping.

"How much do I owe you?" the lawyer asked.

"Counting mileage and parts and time," the plumber said, "that will be $18.00."

"What!" shouted the lawyer. "That's outrageous. Eighteen dollars for ten minutes of work. I'm a lawyer, and I don't make that kind of money."

"Neither did I," said the plumber, "when I was practicing law."

WINSTON K. PENDLETON, *COMPLETE SPEAKER'S GALAXY OF FUNNY STORIES, JOKES AND ANECDOTES*

Signs on a plumber's trucks:
"We repair what your husband fixed."

• • •

"Don't sleep with a drip. Call your plumber."

ANONYMOUS

POLICE OFFICERS:

A policeman spotted a woman who was driving and knitting at the same time.

"Pull over!" he yelled.

"No, officer, it's a scarf."

ANONYMOUS

The Chalk Outline Guy's got a good job. Not too dangerous, the criminals are long gone. I guess these are people who wanted to be sketch artists but they couldn't draw very well.

JERRY SEINFELD

One day a police officer responded to a domestic dispute. Driving up to the apartment building, he heard loud screaming coming from an open window on the second floor. Just as he looked up, a television set came flying out of the window. He proceeded to the apartment and knocked on the door. An angry man shouted out, "Who's there?"

The policeman calmly replied, "TV repairman."

ANONYMOUS

POLITICIANS:

Politicians are interested in people. Not that this is always a virtue. Fleas are interested in dogs.

P. J. O'ROURKE

If God had wanted us to vote, he would have given us candidates.

JAY LENO

PSYCHIATRISTS:

After twelve years of therapy my psychiatrist said something that brought tears to my eyes. He said, "No hablo ingles."

RONNIE SHAKES

A neurotic is the man who builds a castle in the air. A psychotic is the man who lives in it. And a psychiatrist is the man who collects the rents.

ROBERT WEBB-JOHNSTONE

Q: How many psychiatrists does it take to change a light bulb?

A: Only one—but the light bulb has to really want to change.

PAUL DICKSON, *JOKES*

**Anybody who goes to see a psychiatrist
ought to have his head examined.**

SAMUEL GOLDWYN

REALTORS:

**Realtors are people who
did not make it as used car salesmen.**

BOB NEWHART

**I'm sure glad a realtor didn't write Abe Lincoln's
life story. The tiny log cabin would have
become a "rustic country estate."**

BILL JONES

Restaurant Workers:

George had been a waiter all his life. After he died, his wife returned to his restaurant with a psychic to try contacting him in the spirit world. The psychic went into a trance and soon the wife thought she could sense her husband's presence.

"George, George, is that you?" asked the wife.

"Yes, it's me," said a faint voice.

"Come closer, George, I can hardly hear you," she said.

"Sorry," came the reply, "that's not my table."

ANNE KOSTICK, CHARLES FOXGROVER AND
MICHAEL J. PELLOWSKI; *3650 JOKES, PUNS & RIDDLES*

When my son graduated from college he went directly into what I like to call the international food service industry—delivering for a pizzeria.

ROBERT A. ALPER

Sign in a restaurant: Eat now—pay waiter.

ANONYMOUS

Repair Persons:

When our TV went on the fritz, my mother called our small-town repairman. His wife answered and said they were getting a divorce, but she would relay the message since they were still business partners. Later Mom went to the local diner, where townsfolk greeted her. The TV repairman sat in a booth in the back with two other men. When he spied her, he stood up, waved his arms and yelled across the room, "Hey there, not tonight, Mrs. Richter!"

ESTHER BLUMENFELD AND LYNNE ALPERN

88

Salespeople:

Going into a small grocery store, Morty asked, "Do you have any salt?"

"Hoy, salt we have plenty of! Come, I'll show you," said the shopkeeper.

He took Morty into the back room which was filled with salt—13 barrels of salt.

"Wow!" Morty exclaimed. "You really must know how to sell salt."

"Me, no," replied the owner. "I'm not so good at it. But the salesman I bought it from—he can sell salt!"

ANONYMOUS

I was arrested for selling illegal-sized paper.

STEVEN WRIGHT

The sales manager of a big corporation is complaining to his secretary about one of the salesmen. "I tell you, George is so forgetful. It's a wonder he can sell anything. He never remembers anything anybody tells him. I asked him to pick up some cigarettes on his way back from lunch, and I'm not sure he'll even remember to come back!"

All of a sudden the office door flies open and in comes George, the salesman he's talking about.

And the salesman says, "You'll never guess what happened. While I was at lunch, I met old man Brown. He hasn't bought anything from us in five years. Well, we got to talking and by the time we reached dessert, he gave me his half-million dollar order!"

The sales manager turns to his secretary and says, "See, he forgot the cigarettes!"

SOUPY SALES, *STOP ME IF YOU'VE HEARD IT!*

I once worked as a salesman and was very independent.
I took orders from no one.

GERALD BARZAN

Butterfield rented space at one of those outdoor California swap meets. A woman customer picked up a broken fork and asked, "How much?"

"A penny," said Butterfield.

"A penny!" grumbled the woman. "That's too much!"

"Make me an offer."

LARRY WILDE, *LARRY WILDE'S LIBRARY OF LAUGHTER*

A housewife who was slightly hard of hearing answered her doorbell to find a salesman standing there with a large sample case.

"Good morning," he said. "I represent the Amalgamated Woolen Mills. We are offering a special price on a large stock of woolen yarns that didn't come up to our proper standards when it was dyed. The colors ran and the yarns are a bit off color. I'd like to come in and show you my samples."

The woman hadn't understood him very well and said, "I'm sorry, what did you say?"

This time he raised his voice and said, "Would you be interested in some off-colored yarns?"

"I think it would be fun," the lady said. "Come in and we'll have a cup of coffee while you tell them to me."

WINSTON K. PENDLETON, *COMPLETE SPEAKER'S GALAXY OF FUNNY STORIES, JOKES AND ANECDOTES*

STOCKBROKERS:

My father was a very successful businessman but he was
ruined in the stock market crash . . . . A big stockbroker
jumped out the window and fell on his pushcart.

JACKIE MASON

Never invest in anything that eats or needs repairing.

BILLY ROSE

Fantino was legendary in the brokerage business, racking up
commissions that left other brokers in awe. Not only did he
have an incredible sales pitch, he also worked as many as
twenty hours a day.

Eventually, it caught up with him, and he nearly collapsed from
exhaustion. His company insisted that he go into the hospital for
a complete checkup. Fantino complied, but all he could think of
was the commissions he'd be losing while the doctors looked
him over.

The nurse insisted that he lie in bed while they waited for the
doctor. To keep him quiet, she put a thermometer in his mouth.
Ten minutes later, she took it out and looked at it.

"Ninety-seven," she said.

Fantino was looking out the window, his mind elsewhere.
"Good," he mumbled. "When it gets to ninety-nine, sell."

JOE CLARO, *THE RANDOM HOUSE BOOK OF JOKES & ANECDOTES*

Teachers:

Children are stupid. That's why they're in school. I'd lecture for an hour about percentages and interest rates and at the end I'd ask one simple question, "You put ten grand in a bank for one year at five percent and what do you get?" Some kid would always yell out, "A toaster."

FUNINVEST1.COM

One day in heaven, the Lord decided He would visit the earth and take a stroll. Walking down the road, He encountered a man who was crying. The Lord asked the man, "Why are you crying, my son?" The man said that he was blind and had never seen a sunset. The Lord touched the man who could then see and was happy.

As the Lord walked further, He met another man crying and asked, "Why are you crying, my son?" The man was born a cripple and was never able to walk. The Lord touched him and he could walk and he was happy.

Farther down the road, the Lord met another man who was crying and asked, "Why are you crying, my son?" The man said, "Lord, I work for the school system."

And the Lord sat down and cried with him.

ANONYMOUS

Store Clerks:

A woman walked into Rosenfeld's bakery and asked, "How much are bagels?"

"Three twenty-five a dozen," came the reply.

"That's pretty high," said the woman. "Eagerman sells them for two seventy."

"So buy from Eagerman."

"I can't," said the woman. "He's out of bagels."

"Aha!" said Rosenfeld. "When I'm out of bagels, I also sell for two seventy."

WILLIAM NOVAK AND MOSHE WALDOKS, *THE BIG BOOK OF JEWISH HUMOR*

"Good morning. I came to this store because I don't like to bargain."

"Well, you've come to the right place. We're strictly a one-price outfit."

"Excellent. I like that blue suit over there. What will it cost?"

"Like I said, I don't fool around with bargaining. So I'm not going to ask two fifty for this suit, or even two thirty-five. I'm going to give you my best price: two hundred and twenty dollars."

"Well, you're my kind of businessman, and that's why I'm here. I won't fool around and offer you one sixty for that suit, or even one seventy-five. I'll give you two hundred dollars for that suit."

"You can have it for two hundred and ten."

"I'll take it."

SAM LEVINSON

TRAVEL AGENTS:

A woman called a travel agent and asked, "Do airlines put your physical description on your bag so they know whose luggage belongs to who?"

The agent replied, "No, why do you ask?"

The timid-sounding woman said, "Well, when I checked in with the airline, they put a tag on my luggage that said FAT, and I'm overweight. Is there any connection?"

After putting the woman on hold for a minute while she regained her composure, the agent explained to the woman the city code for Fresno is FAT and the airline was just putting a destination tag on her luggage. Makes you wonder if the woman saw the word "terminal" on her luggage, would she have thought she was really sick?

LELAND GREGORY

Sign on a travel agency: We mean it when we say we want you to go away.

ANONYMOUS

WRITERS:

What no wife of a writer can ever understand is that the writer is working when he's staring out the window.

BURTON RASCOE

THE BASIC RULES OF BUSINESS GRAMMAR

1. Use the word "transpire" a lot.

   Wrong: The dog barked.

   Right: What transpired was, the dog barked.

   Even better: A barking of the dog transpired.

2. Also use "parameter."

   Wrong: Employees should not throw paper towels into the toilet.

   Right: Employees should not throw paper towels into parameters of the toilet.

3. Always follow the phrase "Ted and" with the word "myself."

   Wrong: Ted and I think the pump broke.

   Right: Ted and myself think the pump broke.

   Even better: It is the opinion of Ted and myself that a breakage of the pump transpired.

DAVE BARRY

Old accountants never die, they just lose their balance.
Old bankers never die, they just lose interest.
Old bookkeepers never die, they just lose their figures.
Old cashiers never die, they just check out.
Old doctors never die, they just lose their patience.
Old lawyers never die, they just lose their appeal.

SOUPY SALES, *STOP ME IF YOU'VE HEARD IT!*

DOLLARS AND SENSE

Money doesn't always bring happiness. People with ten million are no happier than people with nine million.

HOBART BROWN

Money won't buy happiness, but it will pay the salaries of a large research staff to study the problem.

BILL VAUGHAN

Happiness is a positive cash flow.

ALFRED ADLER

The most popular laborsaving device is still money.

PHYLLIS GEORGE

Right now I have enough money to last me the
rest of my life—unless I buy something.

JACKIE MASON

What, after all is money?
Can you eat it, drink it—make love with it?

WARREN BEATTY

Does anybody believe your health is more important than money?
I don't see too many beautiful women saying, "Hey, should I sleep
with Bill in the Porsche or Dave with low cholesterol?"

NICK DIPAOLO

My boyfriend keeps telling me I've got to own things. So first I
bought this car. And then he told me I ought to get a house. "Why
a house?" "Well, you gotta have a place to park the car."

JULIA ROBERTS

A billion here, a billion there, and pretty
soon you're talking about real money.

EVERETT M. DIRKSEN (ATTRIBUTED)

An old couple came into a giant department store and asked the price. Laughing, the president of the store quoted a price of forty-five million dollars. The man said to his wife, "All right, give me the paper bag you took from under the bed."

The wife handed him the paper sack she was carrying. Dumping the contents on a table, he started counting the bills. Finally it was all counted. It came to forty-one million dollars. The old man sighed and said to his wife, "You brought the wrong paper bag!"

MILTON BERLE, *MILTON BERLE'S PRIVATE JOKE FILE*

Employee No. 1: Ouch!
Employee No. 2: What happened?
Employee No. 1: The edge of my check sliced my finger.
Employee No. 2: Now that's a real pay cut.

ANNE KOSTICK, CHARLES FOXGROVER AND MICHAEL J. PELLOWSKI,
3650 JOKES, PUNS & RIDDLES

When I worked in the computer industry, people often referred to me as a female executive. Is that necessary? I prefer the more politically correct "salary impaired."

JACKIE WOLLNER

SALARY

**He boasted to her
that he pulled in a
six-figure salary.**

**She asked him
if that included
the decimal point.**

CARMEN RICHARDSON RUTLEN

**The boss called in one of his assistants and said,
"I've been told that you went to church and prayed
for a raise. How dare you go over my head!"**

RICHARD S. ZERA, *1001 QUIPS & QUOTES FOR BUSINESS SPEECHES*

**Secretary of Commerce Malcom Baldrige likes to tell how one
high-ranking official once responded to a subordinate's request
for a raise by saying: "Because of the fluctuational predisposition
of your position's productive capacity as juxtaposed to government
standards, it would be monetarily injudicious to advocate an
increment."**
The staff person said, "I don't get it."
The official responded, "That's right."

LOWELL D. STREIKER, *NELSON'S BIG BOOK OF LAUGHTER*

It's amazing how important your job is when you want the day off—and how unimportant it is when you want a raise.

ROBERT ORBEN

Always live within your income,
even if you have to borrow money to do so.

JOSH BILLINGS

Years ago people used to work hard to make both ends meet. With all the payroll deductions today, most of us can't afford two ends.

GENE PERRET

Why is there so much month left at the end of the money?

ANONYMOUS

On income tax day I am reminded that while people say money talks, mine seems to go without saying a word.

MARY ELLEN PINKHAM

SIMPLIFIED TAX FORM

1. How much money did you make last year?
2. Send it in.

ANONYMOUS

The Internal Revenue Service received this letter:

Three years ago I deliberately submitted a false Income Tax Return. Since then, my conscience has bothered me so that I can't sleep well at night. Please apply the enclosed $20 on my past account although the forms do not indicate that I owe it.

At the bottom of the letter was this note:
"PS: If I still can't sleep, I'll send the other $760 later."

WINSTON K. PENDLETON, *COMPLETE SPEAKER'S GALAXY OF FUNNY STORIES, JOKES AND ANECDOTES*

Caller: I got a letter from you guys [the IRS] and I want to know what you want.

IRS: What does it say?

Caller: Just a minute, I'll open it.

• • •

Caller: I'm a bookkeeper and I need to know if ten $100 bills make a thousand dollars or only ten hundred dollars.

IRS: Both. It's the same amount.

Caller: So why do I get a different answer every time I move the decimal point?

• • •

Caller: Could you please send me some of those WD-40's?

COMPILED BY DONNA PATTERSON WILSON

Did you ever notice: when you put the two words
"The" and IRS" together, it spells THEIRS"?

SOUPY SALES, *STOP ME IF YOU'VE HEARD IT!*

You know what a red flag is to the IRS?—
If you have money in your bank accounts after taxes.

JAY LENO

An Internal Revenue agent phoned the local minister and said, "I am going over the return of one of your members. He lists a donation of $3,000 to the church. Can you tell me if he made this contribution?"

The minister said, "I don't have my records before me, but if he didn't, he will."

GASTON FOOTE

Last year, I deducted 10,697 cartons of cigarettes
as a business expense. The tax man said, "Don't ever let
us catch you without a cigarette in your hand."

DICK GREGORY

Mix's Law: There is nothing more permanent than a temporary building. There is nothing more permanent than a temporary tax.

AVERILL Q. MIX

What is the difference between a taxidermist and a tax collector?
The taxidermist takes only your skin.

MARK TWAIN

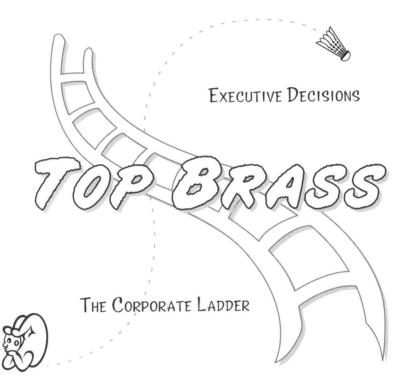

EXECUTIVE DECISIONS

TOP BRASS

THE CORPORATE LADDER

EXECUTIVE DECISIONS

Boss: The man who is early when you are late and late
when you are early.

EVAN ESAR, *ESAR'S COMIC DICTIONARY*

The officers of the company were having a discussion on how
to get employees to work on time. The first vice-president had
this suggestion: "Why don't we reduce the number of employee
parking spaces from 200 to 185?"

All nodded in agreement. "That'll do it," said the president.

RICHARD S. ZERA, *1001 QUIPS & QUOTES FOR BUSINESS SPEECHES*

A guy shows up late for work. The boss yells: "You should
have been here at 7:30 this morning!"

He replies: "Why? What happened at 7:30?"

ANONYMOUS

The boss asked his employees to put suggestions in a box as to
how to improve the business. "When I come in, I like to see
everyone in his or her place having started on the day's work.
Any suggestions?"

The next day there was just one suggestion in the box: "Wear
squeaky shoes."

ANONYMOUS

Boss:	**I'm planning a salary increase.**
Employee:	**Wonderful. When does it become effective?**
Boss:	**As soon as you do.**

PAUL DICKSON, *DICKSON'S JOKE TREASURY*

The boss is a firm believer in fireside chats.
If you don't take his side during a chat, you're fired.

ROBERT ORBEN, *2400 JOKES TO BRIGHTEN YOUR SPEECHES*

My brother-in-law had to give up his last
job because of illness. His boss became sick of him.

HENNY YOUNGMAN

One afternoon an advertising vice-president called the whole staff in to hear a couple of jokes he'd picked up at lunch.

Everybody laughed uproariously except Joyce, who sat there with a glum expression on her face.

The man next to her nudged her and whispered, "What's the matter? Haven't you got a sense of humor?"

"I don't have to laugh," replied Joyce. "I'm quitting Friday."

LARRY WILDE, *LARRY WILDE'S LIBRARY OF LAUGHTER*

During a power outage in our office building my boss was stuck for three hours—on the escalator.

GENE PERRET

A lot of people who complain about their boss being stupid would be out of a job if he were any smarter.

M. C. "CHUCK" COMBS

My supervisor is responsible for three departments, seventy-five employees and five peptic ulcers.

ESTHER BLUMENFELD AND LYNNE ALPERN

The secret of managing is to keep the guys who hate you away from the guys who are undecided.

CASEY STENGEL

By working faithfully eight hours a day, you may eventually get to be a boss and work twelve hours a day.

ROBERT FROST

THE CORPORATE LADDER

The less important you are on the table of organization, the more you'll be missed if you don't show up for work.

BILL VAUGHAN

If all executives were laid end to end, they would not reach a conclusion.

GEORGE BERNARD SHAW (ATTRIBUTED)

The aggressive vice-president was surveying the company's entire operation. He started with the shipping department, walking toward the door of the warehouse. There he saw a young man leaning against a post, reading a newspaper. "How much do you make a week?" he asked the lad.

"Two hundred dollars, Sir," was the reply.

"Here's a week's pay," the executive said. "Now get out!" The executive walked on until he met the foreman. "How long has that kid worked here?" he asked the foreman.

"He doesn't work here . . . he was waiting for a receipt for the merchandise he delivered!"

RICHARD S. ZERA, *1001 QUIPS & QUOTES FOR BUSINESS SPEECHES*

Millionaire: To make it big in business you've got to abide by two principles, honesty and wisdom.

Son: What do you mean, Dad?

Millionaire: Always be honest in business. If you make a promise, keep your word even if you have to go bankrupt to do it.

Son: Okay, Dad. Now what about wisdom?

Millionaire: Wisdom is simple to explain, Son. Never make any promises.

ANNE KOSTICK, CHARLES FOXGROVER AND
MICHAEL J. PELLOWSKI, *3650 JOKES, PUNS & RIDDLES*

SIGNS YOU'VE BEEN IN CORPORATE AMERICA TOO LONG

- Your Valentine's Day cards have bullet points.
- You believe you never have any problems in your life, just "issues" and "improvement opportunities."
- You use the term "value-added" without laughing.

ANONYMOUS

Statistics indicate that, as a result of overwork, modern executives are dropping like flies on the nation's golf courses.

IRA WALLACH

In Japan, the highest-paid executive earns only fifteen times what the average worker does. Here, CEOs earn five hundred times more, but that's supposed to motivate the American worker. To do what, kidnap his boss?

NORMAN K.

My formula for success is rise early, work late, and strike oil.

J. PAUL GETTY

Wives of corporate executives who babble indiscreetly at lunch are a rich source of financial information. Listen carefully and buy them another drink.

DAVID BROWN

A businessman ordered flowers to be sent to the opening of his friend's new branch office. When the businessman got there, he was delighted to see a beautiful floral arrangement. However, he was more than distressed when he read the card that had accompanied the flowers—it read, "Rest in Peace."

He made a beeline to the flower shop and immediately started chewing out the florist. After the shouting had subsided, the florist reassured him by saying, "Hey, don't worry! Just think . . . somewhere today in this city, someone was buried beneath some flowers that read, 'Good luck in your new location!'"

JOEL GOODMAN

The department-store heir Alfred Bloomingdale loved musical comedies and backed a number of Broadway productions, all unsuccessfully. Undeterred by the series of flops, he invested a large sum in a turkey called *Allah Be Praised*. During the disastrous tryout in Boston, Bloomingdale engaged a noted play doctor named Cy Howard who, after sitting through the entire show in silence, finally turned to Bloomingdale and advised, "Al, close the show and keep the store open at night."

JON WINOKUR

SUBTLE SIGNS A COMPANY MAY BE DOWNSIZING

- The traditional Christmas turkey consists of an egg and hatching instructions.

- Your new computer says "Fisher Price" on it.

- The vacation schedule has a notation: "If you feel like staying longer, go for it!"

- Management is passing out "Two-Week Pins" honoring long-term employees.

- At quitting time no one says, "See you tomorrow!"

- You complain to personnel about longer hours, lower pay, less help, lack of benefits, and they respond, "Yeah, so what's your point?"

MARION FOUST

> I don't want any yes-men around me. I want everyone
> to tell me the truth even if it costs them their jobs.
>
> SAMUEL GOLDWYN

MERRY MERGERS

- Xerox and Wurlitzer: They're going to make reproductive organs.

- Fairchild Electronics and Honeywell Computers: New company will be called Fairwell Honeychild.

- Polygram Records, Warner Brothers and Keebler: New company will be called Poly-Warner-Cracker.

- Knott's Berry Farm & National Organization of Women: Knott NOW!

- Fed-Ex & UPS: They will be known as FedUp.

ANONYMOUS

ROAD WARRIORS

UNEMPLOYMENT
INSURANCE

$ ON THE
ROAD AGAIN

GOING-AWAY PARTY

ROAD WARRIORS

Travel is the scourge of the business world. I knew one guy who traveled so much that eventually he wouldn't even park in his own driveway. He thought it was for loading and unloading only . . . .

He's done so much traveling that every time he sits down he puts his seat back and tray table to its upright and locked position.

GENE PERRET

The scientific theory I like best is that the rings of Saturn are composed entirely of lost airline luggage.

MARK RUSSELL

The type of luggage you carry says a lot about you. For example, if you're carrying somebody *else's* luggage, it says you're a thief.

DAVE BARRY

As a professional speaker and trainer, I travel a lot. At the airport one day, I saw a man yelling at the curbside baggage handler. In spite of being barraged with the passenger's anger, the handler remained perfectly calm. After the passenger left the scene, I asked the man how he stayed unruffled in the face of such rage. The airline employee replied, "I just checked his bags in. He's going to Chicago. His bags are going to Japan."

TERRY PAULSON

Late for a flight from Duluth to a conference in Minneapolis, I arrived just in time to dash aboard. Buckling up, I noticed I was the only passenger on the 737 jet, with seven flight attendants. After take-off I surreptitiously got permission to use the microphone: "Attention flight crew, this is your passenger speaking . . . . "

ESTHER BLUMENFELD AND LYNNE ALPERN

Whenever I travel I like to keep the seat next to me empty.
I found a great way to do it. When someone walks down
the aisle and says to you, "Is someone sitting there?"
just say, "No one—except the Lord."

CAROL LEIFER

You should definitely have a travel agent.
Why go through all the hassle of dealing with airlines,
hotels, and rental-car agencies yourself, only to see the
arrangements get all screwed up, when with just
a single phone call you can have a trained
professional screw them up for you?

DAVE BARRY

If God wanted us to fly, he would have given us tickets.

MEL BROOKS

If the Lord had wanted people to fly, He would have
made it simpler for people to get to the airport.

MILTON BERLE

Most hotel keys are now the shape of a credit card.
One night I got back to my room late and accidentally used my
Visa card, and the next month I got billed for a hotel door.

DOBIE MAXWELL

I was at a place called the Fractured Arms . . . . You can imagine
how big my room was—when I closed the door, the doorknobs got
in bed with me. It was so small, even the mice were hunchback.

HENNY YOUNGMAN

Generally speaking, the length and grandness of a hotel's name are an exact opposite reflection of its quality. Thus the Hotel Central will prove to be a clean, pleasant place in a good part of town, and the Hotel Royal Majestic-Fantastic will be a fleabag next to a topless bowling alley.

MISS PIGGY

UNEMPLOYMENT INSURANCE

I lost my job. No, not really. I know where my job is. It's just that when I go there, a new guy is doing it.

BOBCAT GOLDTHWAIT

Tafel worked for a Rhode Island company for twenty-five years, then was let go. He asked for a letter of recommendation and the employer wrote this for him:

TO WHOM IT MAY CONCERN: Mr. R. Tafel worked for us for twenty-five years and when he left we were perfectly satisfied.

LARRY WILDE, *LARRY WILDE'S LIBRARY OF LAUGHTER*

According to the latest statistics, there are five million Americans who aren't working. And there are plenty more if you count the ones with jobs.

ANONYMOUS

Unemployment is a tough thing. Even if you get a job, they take unemployment out of your check every week, and show it to you in that little box. How good can it be for your confidence that every paycheck has got the word "unemployment" on it? You can't get it out of your head. You just got the job, they're already getting ready for you to get laid off!

JERRY SEINFELD

The trouble with unemployment is that the minute you wake up in the morning you're on the job.

SLAPPY WHITE

GOING-AWAY PARTY

Retiree: A member of the leisure class.

EVAN ESAR, *ESAR'S COMIC DICTIONARY*

When a colleague retires, it's not considered good form to snatch his chair while he's still in it.

ESTHER BLUMENFELD AND LYNNE ALPERN

When a man retires, the wife gets twice the husband, but only half the income.

CHI CHI RODRIGUEZ

The pension is mightier than the sword.

ANONYMOUS

Look before you leap. Before you retire,
stay home for a week and watch daytime television.

FRED METCALF, *THE PENGUIN DICTIONARY OF JOKES*

The problem with retirement is that you
can't leave all of your problems at the office.

RICHARD S. ZERA, *1001 QUIPS & QUOTES FOR BUSINESS SPEECHES*

When leaving office, give your successor three sealed envelopes
and instructions to open them in order as crises occur in the new
administration. The message in the first should read "blame it on
your predecessors," the second should read "announce a major
reorganization," and the third should say, "write out three
envelopes for your successor."

JAMES GLEASON

At his retirement ceremony the boss told him, "The way we see it,
we're not so much losing a worker as gaining a parking space."

FRED METCALF, *THE PENGUIN DICTIONARY OF JOKES*

A vacationing banker was at the dock of a small coastal village when a fisherman tied up his small boat. He had several large yellow fin tuna. The banker complimented the fisherman, "Good looking fish. How long did it take to catch them?"

The fisherman replied, "Only a little while."

"So why didn't you stay at sea longer to catch more fish?" asked the banker.

The fisherman replied, "These are enough to support my family's needs."

The banker then asked, "But what do you do with the rest of your time?"

The fisherman said, "I sleep late, relax, spend time with my family, hang out with friends."

The banker scoffed, "I am a Harvard MBA and could help you. If you would spend more time fishing, you could buy a bigger boat. With the bigger boat you would catch even more fish and so buy more boats; eventually you would have a fleet. Then you could sell directly to the processor, maybe even open your own cannery. Eventually you would control the product, processing and distribution. You could leave this small village and live anywhere: Los Angeles, New York City, London."

The fisherman quietly asked, "How long will this all take?" To which the banker replied, "15 to 20 years."

"But what then?"

The banker laughed, "That's the best part! When the time is right, you sell your company stock to the public and become very rich. You could make millions!"

"Millions," replied the fisherman. "And then what?"

"Then you could retire. Move to a small village on the sea where you'd do nothing but sleep late, relax, spend time with your family, hang out with your friends."

ANONYMOUS

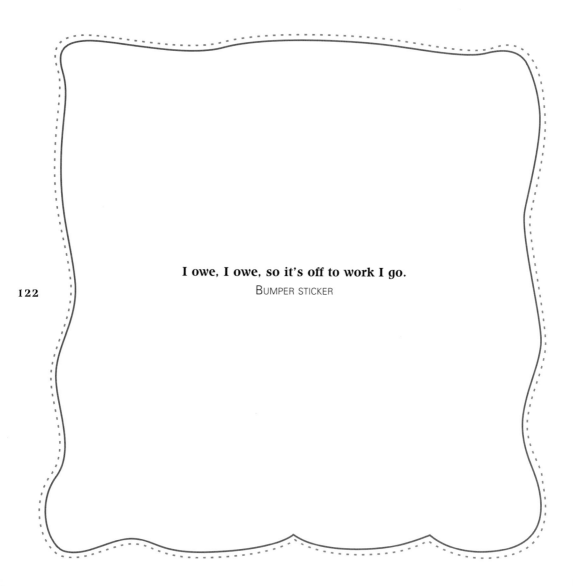

I owe, I owe, so it's off to work I go.

BUMPER STICKER

122

INDEX

123

125

127

ABOUT THE AUTHOR

Allen Klein is the world's only "Jollytologist." He is an award-winning professional speaker, best-selling author, and the President of the Association for Applied and Therapeutic Humor (www.aath.org). Klein teaches people worldwide how to use humor to deal with not-so-funny stuff. In addition to this book and two others in the series—*ParentLaughs* and *TeacherLaughs*—he is also the author of *Up Words for Down Days, The Change-Your-Life Quote Book, The Lift-Your-Spirits Quote Book, The Celebrate-Your-Life Quote Book, The Simplify-Your-Life Quote Book, The Love and Kisses Quote Book, The Wise and Witty Quote Book*, and *Reflections on Life: Why We're Here and How to Enjoy the Journey*, among others.

For more information about Klein or his presentations go to www.allenklein.com, or, e-mail him at humor@allenklein.com